INTRODUCTION

'The world in one country' is a label often used to describe the variety of landscape within New Zealand, and arguably no other place on the planet could claim such diversity in the same compact area. Nearly every type of natural geographical feature can be found, from glaciers, fiords and rainforests in the south to live volcanoes, drowned river systems and sub-tropical beaches in the north. Many of the best natural features are protected within a comprehensive system of national parks and reserves.

New Zealand boasts modern cities in stunning locations. The largest city, Auckland, embraces the yacht-filled Waitemata Harbour; Wellington clings to steep hillsides with exquisite views over Wellington Harbour; the peaceful Avon River meanders through the South Island city of Christchurch, located beside the Pacific Ocean and under the Southern Alps; and in the deep south, Dunedin occupies a natural amphitheatre at the end of Otago Harbour.

The Maori, the first people to settle, arrived in Aotearoa (land of the long white cloud) in the 14th century and have retained a strong presence within contemporary New Zealand culture. The next wave of settlers came from Europe, particularly Britain, in the 19th and 20th centuries. More recently immigrants have come from the Pacific Islands and Asia, mainly to the Auckland region. New Zealanders have a proud heritage of being resourceful and inventive, and are known for their open friendliness and love of sport and adventure.

Many of New Zealand's wildlife and flora species including the kiwi, the national symbol, are unique due to the isolation in which they have evolved. New Zealand is one of the few countries with no land species considered dangerous to humans and this, combined with a mild climate and stunningly beautiful scenery, has attracted another commonly used label – that of 'God's own county'.

LEFT The Pacific Ocean and the Tasman Sea meet at Cape Reinga, the north-western tip of the North Island.

BELOW Ahipara Bay, with its magnificent sandy dunes seen here in the background, is located at the south end of Ninety Mile Beach.

RIGHT TOP The strong straight trunks of centuries-old kauri trees have long been prized for their timber, but nowadays these specimens in Northland's Waipoua Forest are protected.

RIGHT BELOW The 'Hole in the Rock' at Motukokako Island is a popular destination for ferries and pleasure boats in the Bay of Islands.

Left Top The idyllic town of Russell in the Bay of Islands attracts tourists as well as those intent on catching big game fish.

Far Left Below A sea kayaker paddles through a tunnel of mangroves at high tide near Northland's historic settlement of Waitangi.

Left Below New Zealand's oldest stone building, the Stone Store near Kerikeri, was completed in 1835.

Above The Town Basin in Whangarei, Northland's major centre, is the ideal base for the many yachts that cruise Northland's scenic coastline.

Right Gulf Harbour Marina at Whangaparaoa Peninsula, north of Auckland, offers boaties and residents of this upmarket canal village ready access to the many islands of the Hauraki Gulf.

ABOVE The extraordinary view from Auckland's Sky Tower over Auckland city, Waitemata Harbour, the North Shore suburb of Devonport, and out to the low volcanic cone of Rangitoto Island.

LEFT As well as being a sophisticated business centre, today Auckland city is a melting pot of different cultures with particularly strong influences from the Pacific Islands and, more recently, Asia.

RIGHT Only a 30-minute ferry ride from Auckland City, Waiheke Island is fast gaining recognition for its boutique wines and olive oils while retaining its appeal for alternative lifestylers and as a holiday destination.

LEFT TOP Prior to the 1999/2000 America's Cup challenge, Auckland's Viaduct Basin area underwent a major refurbishment and now boasts an impressive range of cafés and bars.

LEFT BELOW Auckland's Harbour Bridge provides an attractive backdrop to Westhaven Marina. Given the number of boats berthed here, it's easy to see how Auckland came by its nickname of 'City of Sails'.

RIGHT TOP The lush sub-tropical forest of the Waitakere Ranges in west Auckland is just 40 minutes' drive from the city.

RIGHT CENTRE A short ferry ride across Waitemata Harbour from central Auckland is the North Shore village of Devonport, where one can enjoy a coffee, wine or beer at a more leisurely pace.

RIGHT BELOW Sitting prominently atop Auckland Domain is the Auckland Museum. The impressive building was completed in 1929 as a memorial to those who died in World War I.

LEFT AND ABOVE Visitors to the limestone caves at Waitomo, a spectacular underground network 75 km south-west of Hamilton, can take part in a number of caving-related activities including abseiling.

BELOW The paddle steamer MV *Waipa Delta* makes excursions up and down New Zealand's longest river, the Waikato. The excursions leave from Hamilton, the North Island's third-largest city.

PREVIOUS PAGES The outlook from Paku Hill on the Coromandel Peninsula affords great views of Tairua Harbour and the town of Pauanui, a weekend retreat for many well-to-do Aucklanders.

LEFT TOP The seaside town of Whitianga, situated on the eastern side of the Coromandel Peninsula, is popular with holiday-makers, boaties, and deep sea fishermen.

LEFT CENTRE Clear, sparkling waters surge around the Cathedral Cove rock formation near Hahei on the Coromandel Peninsula.

LEFT BELOW At the entrance to Tauranga Harbour on the east coast, the volcanic cone of Mount Maunganui overlooks the town of the same name.

RIGHT TOP From the top of Mount Maunganui there are great views of the township bound by Tauranga Harbour on one side and the Pacific Ocean on the other.

RIGHT BELOW Although White Island in the Bay of Plenty is an active volcano, it poses little threat to the mainland as it is some 50 km off the coast.

LEFT A raft plunges over Tutea's Falls, part of the series of rapids and falls that make up Okere Falls, on the Kaituna River near Rotorua.

BELOW Rotorua's Museum of Art and History, more commonly known as 'The Bath House' because of its original function as a spa retreat, is situated in that city's Government Gardens.

Above As well as entertaining and educating tourists, The New Zealand Maori Arts and Crafts Institute in Rotorua also trains local Maori in wood and greenstone carving and cultural performance.

Right and Below Rotorua's many and varied thermally active sites – including boiling mud pools, geysers, steam vents, and colourful thermal pools – have made the region the North Island's most popular tourist destination.

LEFT TOP Snow-capped mountains and the central North Island lake and township of Taupo make a spectacular backdrop for the Huka Falls (foreground), formed by the Waikato River dropping some 8 metres over a rock ledge.

LEFT BELOW Also in the central North Island, the Tongariro River draws anglers keen to try their luck from all around the world.

ABOVE On the approach leading up to the volcanic cone of Mount Ngauruhoe, a sign warns motorists to watch out for kiwi, the flightless bird that is New Zealand's national symbol.

RIGHT Whakapapa, the North Island's major ski field, is situated on the slopes of Mount Ruapehu. In 1995 skiers and snowboarders on the field had excellent views of this active volcano's eruption, although ash fallout later temporarily closed the ski area.

PREVIOUS PAGES Lake Taupo, New Zealand's largest lake, is a holiday and tourist centre offering a variety of outdoor activities including world famous trout fishing.

LEFT TOP The Waioeka Gorge in eastern Bay of Plenty cuts through a rugged landscape of native bush between the Urewera National Park and Raukumara Forest Park.

LEFT BELOW A marae (Maori village or settlement and its buildings) on the North Island's East Cape. The distinctive carvings are a common sight in this region.

RIGHT Every year about 10 000 Australasian Gannets come to breed at the massive cliffs at Cape Kidnappers in Hawke's Bay.

BELOW The east coast city of Gisborne is known for its warm, sunny climate and relaxed pace of life.

ABOVE AND LEFT After a massive earthquake devastated the Hawke's Bay city of Napier in 1931, much of the city was rebuilt in the art deco style of the time.

ABOVE The Hawke's Bay region's high quality produce and award-winning wines make it a very attractive destination for visitors with a serious interest in wine and food.

RIGHT Martinborough in the Wairarapa has also made a name for itself through its wine-making activities. This hotel is a very popular place to stay, especially during the town's annual wine festival.

PREVIOUS PAGES AND ABOVE The impressive 2518 m volcanic cone that dominates the Taranaki countryside and the city of New Plymouth is known as Taranaki/Mount Egmont.

LEFT The Whanganui River, 290 km long, was an important early transport route. An historic paddleboat still plies the river, today carrying tourists rather than supplies.

OPPOSITE TOP LEFT The white cliffs of the North Taranaki Bight fringe the fertile Taranaki plains.

OPPOSITE TOP RIGHT A paraglider pilot flies high over the Kapiti Coast, north of Wellington. In the distance is the bird sanctuary of Kapiti Island.

OPPOSITE BELOW Wellington, New Zealand's capital city, comprises the country's second-largest urban area.

Left and Above Property in Wellington's marine suburb of Oriental Bay is in high demand as it not only commands some magnificent views, but is just a few minutes' walk from the central business district.

Right Wellington's cable car has been taking passengers up the hill to the pleasant suburb of Kelburn since 1902. En route it makes several stops, but it is at the very top where the best views over the city and harbour can be seen.

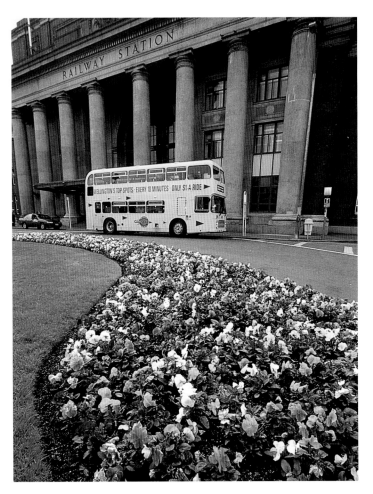

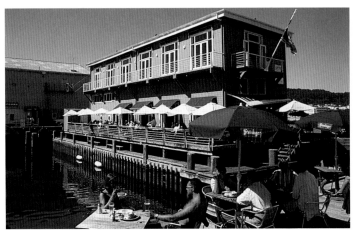

LEFT TOP Yellow double-decker buses offer regular tours of the city starting from Wellington Railway Station. The station is an important transport hub, as a substantial number of the city's workers commute from outlying areas.

LEFT CENTRE Popular eateries like Café L'Affare have helped establish Wellington's reputation as the 'café capital' of the country.

LEFT BELOW On Wellington's waterfront historic warehouses have been turned into cafés, restaurants and bars – perfect for enjoying the capital's balmy summer days.

RIGHT TOP AND BELOW Te Papa Tongarewa, the impressive Museum of New Zealand, was opened in 1998. It has a huge range of displays over a wide variety of subject matter including history, culture, artworks, natural history and an interactive section.

PREVIOUS PAGES The complex of bays, channels, sounds, peninsulas and islands that make up the Marlborough Sounds at the northern tip of the South Island make it one of New Zealand's most picturesque holiday destinations.

ABOVE Picton, a small seaside town on Queen Charlotte Sound, is the gateway to the South Island for the many visitors who arrive via the Cook Strait ferry.

LEFT Ferns abound on the many walking tracks that wind through the forest parks in this part of the South Island.

TOP Many award-winning wines, including New Zealand's internationally acclaimed sauvignon blanc, are produced in the Marlborough region.

ABOVE AND RIGHT The scenic town of Kaikoura in southern Marlborough has become famous as a place to view marine mammals, such as whales, dolphins and seals.

LEFT AND ABOVE The graceful curve of Farewell Spit extends eastward from Cape Farewell, the north-western extremity of the South Island. Spectacular sandstone cliffs and rock arches feature on the remote coast immediately south of the cape itself.

BELOW This quaint looking general store at Bainham, Golden Bay, supplies trampers near the northern end of the Heaphy Track.

LEFT AND BELOW Outdoor activities among the idyllic bays, islands and inlets of Abel Tasman National Park include exploring the forest and coastal tracks, and sea kayaking in the pristine waters.

ABOVE The main access point to the picturesque Nelson Lakes National Park is from the village of St Arnaud, situated on the shores of Lake Rotoiti.

RIGHT River rafters appreciate the natural scenery between sections of frenzied white water on the Buller, the major river on the South Island's West Coast.

ABOVE The South Island's majestic
Southern Alps rear above the West
Coast.

LEFT At high tide water is forced –
with spectacular results – through
blowholes in the Pancake Rocks at
Punakaiki in Paparoa National Park
on the West Coast.

ABOVE Shantytown on the West Coast was built specifically as a tourist attraction to portray many aspects typical of early mining towns.

RIGHT The high annual rainfall received by Paparoa National Park on the West Coast has produced a luxuriant subtropical rain forest that includes ferns and nikau palms – the world's southernmost palm tree.

LEFT Day hikers are guided through the crevasses of the 14 km long Fox Glacier in the South Island's Westland/Tai Poutini National Park.

BELOW Franz Josef Glacier is in the same National Park as the Fox Glacier. These are two of the most accessible glaciers in the world.

RIGHT TOP Mueller Hut on Sealy Range affords great views of the mountains of Aoraki/Mount Cook National Park, including Mount Sefton, seen here above the clouds.

RIGHT BELOW A South Island tour bus makes its way slowly through a flock of sheep, towered over by New Zealand's highest mountain, Aoraki/Mount Cook.

PREVIOUS PAGES The small stone Church of the Good Shepherd looks out over Lake Tekapo and the Two Thumb Range in the Mackenzie Country, South Canterbury.

ABOVE Rock climbing is a popular sport on the unusual rock formations of Canterbury's Castle Hill.

LEFT The TranzAlpine Express route offers stunning views of the Southern Alps and surrounding environs.

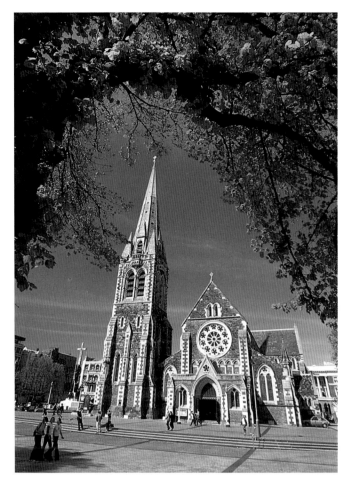

ABOVE Cathedral Square in the centre of Christchurch, the South Island's largest city, is named after the Cathedral Church of Christ, which was completed in 1904 after a 40-year construction period.

ABOVE RIGHT A punter and passengers pole along the Avon River in park-like surroundings in downtown Christchurch, a world away from the busy business district surrounding them.

RIGHT The French influences still evident today in the small town of Akaroa on Akaroa Harbour, Banks Peninsula, came about because this area was originally settled by French immigrants back in 1840.

LEFT A hot air balloon appears to fill the sky. It's a popular activity on the wide flat expanse of the Canterbury Plains.

BELOW Autumn's glorious tones are reflected in Lake Benmore, a man-made lake in Otago's Waitaki Valley.

RIGHT TOP Hay for winter feed dots this part of the Canterbury Plains. Such numbers of crops are grown here that the plains are often called the South Island's 'bread-basket'.

RIGHT BELOW Oamaru in North Otago is known for its historic buildings made from locally quarried white sandstone. Every November the town celebrates it heritage with numerous events including penny farthing races.

LEFT The unusual concretions known as the Moeraki Boulders on the north Otago coast were formed some 60 million years ago when lime minerals gradually accumulated around fossil shells or bones.

BELOW Dunedin is well known for its fine historic architecture, much of it built on the proceeds of the Otago gold rush of the late 1800s. The city's railway station is an exceptional example of the period.

Above The Octagon forms a centre piece for the city of Dunedin. The city is formed around the head of the 25 km long Otago Harbour on the eroded walls of an ancient volcanic crater.

Above Right A Royal Albatross from the Taiaroa Head colony near Dunedin on Otago Peninsula is inspected by a wildlife ranger. The colony is unique as it is the only one in the world on a mainland or near a major human population.

Right A hang glider, looking not unlike the huge-winged albatross in flight, soars high above Hoopers Inlet on Otago Peninsula.

Previous Pages Few vineyards anywhere could match Rippon Vineyard beside Lake Wanaka for its stunning location.

Above The Shotover Jet takes tourists on a spectacular ride through the canyons of the Shotover River, a few kilometres outside of Queenstown.

Left Commercial bungy jumping was pioneered by New Zealander A.J. Hackett, and the world's first commercial bungy site is the historic suspension bridge across the Kawarau River near Queenstown.

ABOVE Gondolas take passengers high up on to Bob's Peak above Queenstown to admire views over Lake Wakatipu and The Remarkables. The more adventurous can return to Queenstown via a tandem paraglider flight.

BELOW The Central Otago town of Cromwell on the shores of the recently formed Lake Dunstan.

LEFT TOP Some of the alpine slopes near Lake Wanaka are ideal for extreme skiing events.

LEFT BELOW A relic from the gold rush of the 1860s in the Central Otago ghost town of Stewart Town, near Bannockburn.

RIGHT TOP The longest of the South Island lakes, Wakatipu is a deep glacial lake surrounded by mountains.

RIGHT CENTRE AND BELOW The quaint little settlement of Arrowtown was built during the gold rush of the late 1800s. Unlike Queenstown, 20 km away, it has experienced little architectural change over more than a century.

LEFT Nugget Point, one of the more spectacular points on the South Otago coastline, is home to numerous marine species including New Zealand fur seals and various species of penguin.

BELOW Sheep graze above Tautuku Bay in the remote Catlins district. This part of the southern coastline is known for its deserted beaches, rocky outcrops and very few human inhabitants.

RIGHT TOP New Zealand sea lions are regular visitors to Cannibal Bay in the Catlins.

RIGHT BELOW Matai Falls is one of a number of beautiful waterfalls scattered throughout the native forests of the Catlins district.

ABOVE Dusky Sound on the South Island's south-western corner remains as rugged and inaccessible by land as it was in Captain Cook's time.

BELOW AND OPPOSITE Milford Road in Cleddau Valley, and Mitre Peak, Milford Sound, are part of the magnificent Fiordland National Park, which in turn makes up a major part of the Te Wahipounamu South-West New Zealand World Heritage Area.

Above The sheer splendour of Milford Sound is admired by visitors on board the *Milford Wanderer*.

Below Although known for its oysters and its proximity to Stewart Island, the southern township of Bluff is a long way from everywhere else in the world.